445

Has

Count Your Way through
Italy

by Jim Haskins

illustrations by Beth Wright

Carolrhoda Books, Inc./Minneapolis

To Brenan and Banyon. —J.H.

This book is available in two editions:
Library binding by Carolrhoda Books, Inc.
Soft cover by First Avenue Editions
c/o The Lerner Group
241 First Avenue North
Minneapolis, Minnesota 55401

LIBRARY OF CONGRESS CATALOGING-IN-PUBLICATION DATA

Haskins, James, 1941-
    Count your way through Italy / by Jim Haskins ; illustrated by
Beth Wright.
        p.   cm.
    Summary: Uses the numbers one through ten in Italian to introduce
aspects of the history and culture of Italy.
    ISBN 0-87614-406-7 (lib. bdg.)
    ISBN 0-87614-533-0 (pbk.)
    1. Italy—Civilization—Juvenile literature. 2. Counting—
Juvenile literature. [1. Italy—Civilivation. 2. Counting.
3. Italian language materials—Bilingual.] I. Wright, Beth, ill.
II. Title.
DG441.H37   1990
945—dc20
[E]   89-37455

Manufactured in the United States of America
4 5 6 7 8 9 – P/SP – 01 00 99 98 97 96

Introductory Note

Italian developed from Latin, the language of the ancient Romans. Thus, it is called a "Romance" language. (Two other Romance languages are French and Spanish.)

Italian uses the same alphabet as English, but the letters are often pronounced differently. The final *e* in Italian is usually pronounced like *ay* as in *bay*, and the final *i* is pronounced like *ee* as in *bee*. In Italian, an *e* or an *i* is used at the end of a noun to make it plural, unlike English, where an *s* or *es* is used. There are accents in the Italian language, but there are none in the numbers we will be learning.

1 uno (OO-no)

There is only **one** Mount Etna, the largest and highest volcano in Europe. One of the world's major active volcanoes, Mount Etna's most recent eruption took place in 1983. Although the volcano's height and crater dimensions constantly change, its highest point is above 11,100 feet (3,390 m.). Mount Etna is located on the offshore Italian island of Sicily.

The name of the volcano comes from a Greek word meaning "I burn." Thousands of years ago, the people of nearby Greece created many myths about Mount Etna. One was that a giant named Typhon lay buried underneath it. When Typhon struggled to escape, the Earth would tremble, and the giant's breath would explode from the volcano in bursts of flame and smoke.

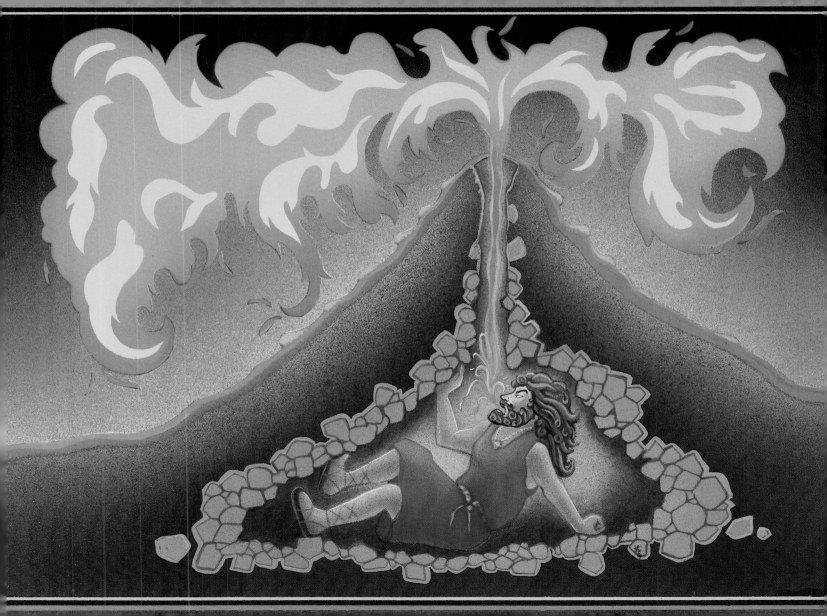

2 due (DOO-ay)

According to ancient Roman tradition, **two** brothers named Romulus and Remus founded Rome, the capital of Italy. Legend has it that the twins were the sons of Mars, the god of war, and were raised by a wolf. The brothers set out together to start a new city. In a fit of rivalry over who should choose the site, Romulus killed Remus. And so, the story goes, he named the city Rome after himself, the victor.

3 tre (tray)

Italian Christopher Columbus (Cristoforo Colombo) sailed **three** ships to the New World in 1492. The rulers of Spain supplied the Spanish ships the *Niña*, the *Pinta*, and the *Santa María* for Columbus's voyage of discovery. Columbus himself sailed on the *Santa María*, but his favorite ship is said to have been the *Niña*. When the *Santa María* sank off the coast of Haiti on Christmas Day, 1492, Columbus moved over to the *Niña*. It was on this ship that he sailed safely home.

4 quattro (KWAHT-troh)

Four rows of columns make up the two colonnades that ring the *piazza* (pee-AH-tsah), or square, in front of Saint Peter's Church, the largest church in the world. They were designed by the Italian architect Gian Lorenzo Bernini in the 1600s.

St. Peter's Church is located inside the Vatican City, which is an independent state within the city of Rome. The Pope, the world leader of the Catholic faith, lives in the Vatican City, and it is here that the most important business of the Catholic Church is conducted.

ITALY

Venice

Rome

Sicily

5 cinque (CHEEN-kway)

In one of the many *Adventures of Pinocchio*, Fire-eater the puppet-master gives Pinocchio **five** gold pieces. Instead of taking the money home to his father, Gepetto, Pinocchio goes off with the Fox and the Cat. There are many more adventures of Pinocchio, including the Pinocchio story made famous by Walt Disney Productions.

Italy's Carlo Collodi created the character of Pinocchio more than a century ago. He may have chosen to write a story about a puppet because of the great popularity of puppetry in Italy, where it has delighted young and old for centuries.

6 sei (say)

There are **six** main districts in the Italian city of Venice, most of which lies on over 100 islands in the Adriatic Sea. Venice is famous for the *gondola* (GOHN-doh-lah), which is a flat-bottomed boat propelled by long oars. More modern is the *vaporetto* (vah-poh-REHT-toh), or motorboat bus.

Some of the world's finest art and architecture can be found in Venice. Because the entire city is surrounded by seawater, Venice has been troubled by flooding and erosion. In the 1970s, people from all over the world worked together to halt the flooding, which was causing Venice and its priceless art treasures to sink slowly into the sea.

7 sette (SEHT-tay)

Seven foods that are associated with Italy are: pizza (which originated in Naples), Parmesan cheese, mozzarella cheese, pasta (spaghetti and macaroni, for example), prosciutto (dry-cured ham), marinara (a tomato sauce), and salami.

Italians spend more money per person on food than people in any other Western European country. Instead of using frozen and canned foods, they prefer to shop daily to get the freshest food possible. Carefully prepared food and the eating of meals together are important aspects of Italian family life.

8 otto (OHT-to)

Eight characters can be found in the *Commedia dell'arte* (kohm-MAY-dee-ah dehl AHR-tay), a form of theater that flourished in Italy from the sixteenth to the eighteenth century. The same cast of characters is used in a variety of situations for each play.

The most famous character was Arlecchino, an acrobat and a wit who was prone to falling in love. He wore a black, catlike mask and clothes of many colors, which later were patterned in red, green, and blue diamonds. This is the origin of the Harlequin image.

While Commedia dell'arte has not been regularly performed in Italy since the early part of the eighteenth century, its influence on Italian drama can still be seen.

9 nove (NO-vay)

Nine products for which Italy is known are: leather goods, sports cars, high-fashion clothing, contemporary furnishings, movies, marble, wine, olive oil, and cheese. The manufactured products, which come mainly from the north, are admired for their superiority of design and style. The agricultural products, which come mainly from the south, are equally admired for their quality.

10 dieci (DYAY-chee)

Ten horses are chosen to race in the Corsa del Palio (KOHR-sah dehl PAH-lee-oh) in the Italian city of Siena twice each summer. The Palio is a long silk banner that is the prize for the winning horse. The Palio race is a descendant of ancient games going back to the ancient Romans. The race is preceded by a parade in which men dress up as warriors in flexible armor made of metal links, called chain mail. Women wear black gowns, and everyone waves colorful banners.

Pronunciation Guide

1 / **uno** / (OO-no)
2 / **due** / (DOO-ay)
3 / **tre** / (tray)
4 / **quattro** / (KWAHT-troh)
5 / **cinque** / (CHEEN-kway)
6 / **sei** / (say)
7 / **sette** / (SEHT-tay)
8 / **otto** / (OHT-to)
9 / **nove** / (NO-vay)
10 / **dieci** / (DYAY-chee)